Sarah Clarke

Herbert t
Hedgeho

GOES ON HOLIDAY

Story by John and Linda Kelham
Illustrated by 'Riggers'

HIPPO

Hippo Books
Scholastic Publications Limited
London

Scholastic Publications Ltd.,
10 Earlham Street, London WC2H 9LN, U.K.

Scholastic Inc.,
730 Broadway, New York, NY 10003, USA

Scholastic Tab Publications Ltd.,
123 Newkirk Road, Richmond Hill,
Ontario L4C 3G5, Canada

Ashton Scholastic Pty. Ltd.,
P O Box 579, Gosford, New South Wales,
Australia

Ashton Scholastic Ltd.,
165 Marua Road, Panmure, Auckland 6,
New Zealand

First published by Scholastic Publications Ltd., 1986

ISBN 0 590 70533 4

Made and printed in Spain by Mateu Cromo, Madrid
Typeset in plantin

It was a lovely sunny day in the middle of spring.

Herbert the hedgehog was busily packing his suitcases. Today he was going on holiday with his parents.

They were going to stay with Mrs Spike's sister and her family, who had recently moved to Sunnyvale-by-the-Sea.

Herbert always enjoyed seeing his cousins, Bertie and Betsy, and was especially looking forward to his first visit to the seaside.

"I hope you've packed everything you need Herbert," said Mrs Spike.

"Oh so do I," he exclaimed, and all three rode off merrily on their bicycles.

Mr and Mrs Spike kept a watchful eye on Herbert, making sure that he didn't race too far ahead.

After a long ride through the very narrow country lanes, they arrived at Auntie Harriet's and Uncle George's cottage.

Mr Spike rang the door bell and they all waited patiently.

"Hello, how lovely to see you," said Herbert's auntie. "Do come inside."

They all walked into the little cottage.

"Where are Bertie and Betsy?" asked Herbert excitedly. "I hope they haven't forgotten that I'm coming."

"Oh no, of course not," said Aunt Harriet. "They are outside playing – I'll call them in."

"Bertie! Betsy!" called out Auntie Harriet. The little hedgehogs came running in from the garden.

"Hello Herbert, how are you?" asked Bertie.

"It's lovely to see you again," said Betsy. "We always have such fun when you come to stay."

Auntie Harriet brought in the lunch and they all sat down to their favourite meal of crispy salad with nuts and home-made apple pie.

When they had eaten everything, Bertie, Betsy and Herbert went outside to explore.

"Come on," urged Herbert. "You can show me the sea."

Now Herbert had never seen the sea before. He was very excited and began to sing . . .

"Hi diddlee dee,
we're off to see the sea.
Hi diddlee dum,
we're bound to have some fun."

“Where are you off to, this bright and sunny afternoon?” came a voice from above.

Herbert looked up to see a bird sitting in a tree.

“Hello little bird,” said Herbert. “That’s a good question!”

Herbert looked at the others. “Well there’s three of us and we must be going somewhere. That’s it — we’re going shopping.”

“No we’re not, you silly hedgehog,” laughed Betsy. “We’re going to the beach.”

“Oh yes, now I remember,” said Herbert. “Silly me.”

“Look at all that sand,” said Bertie. “Have you ever seen anything like it before?”

“No I haven’t,” Herbert replied. “And look at all those young humans building castles and digging holes.”

Herbert, Betsy and Bertie raced down to the sea.

They watched spellbound as the huge waves crashed down onto the beach.

"Ouch! That's cold," exclaimed Herbert, as some water splashed onto him. "I don't think I'll go swimming today."

Just then, something caught his eye. Farther up the beach a crowd of children was gathered.

Herbert was very curious to see what was going on.

Now hedgehogs are usually wary of humans, but Herbert was so curious that he crept closer to investigate.

What he saw made him blink. There, just in front of the children, was a little striped tent.

Herbert stood watching for a few minutes. He looked back and saw that Bertie and Betsy had dozed off in the sunshine.

"They're missing all the fun," thought Herbert to himself.

PUNCH AND JUDY

Suddenly, two funny-looking characters appeared from a hole in the front of the tent.

Written at the top of the tent were the words PUNCH AND JUDY.

"Whatever can it be?" Herbert wondered.

What he saw made him quite worried. Punch and Judy were having a fight, and one of them seemed to be getting hurt.

"I must do something to help," said Herbert, as he edged nearer the tent.

In his excitement Herbert quite forgot his fear of humans.

He climbed up through the opening in the tent and landed between Punch and Judy.

The children went wild with excitement.

"Look, a hedgehog's come to the rescue!" called out a voice from the audience.

What a funny sight it was to see Herbert on the stage.

"There isn't usually a hedgehog in a Punch and Judy show," called out a puzzled child.

Herbert tried to stop the fight, not realizing they were puppets.

All of a sudden Herbert felt a thump on his head. Punch had hit him with his hammer, thinking he was Judy.

The blow sent poor Herbert tumbling from the stage. He scuttled off in fright.

The children started shouting:
"We want the hedgehog! We want the hedgehog!"

The man who was doing the Punch and Judy show couldn't understand why they were shouting.

"There was no hedgehog," Punch called out to the children.

"Oh yes there was!" chorused the children.

"Oh no there wasn't!"
shouted Punch.

Herbert hurried back to Bertie and Betsy, holding his head which still hurt from the blow.

"Wake up!" shouted Herbert, shaking them.

They both woke up with a start.

"You'll never guess what happened," gasped Herbert.

Bertie and Betsy heard the childrens' voices shouting in the distance.

"Quick," cried Bertie. "We'd better go home — the children must be after us."

"I can't think why," chuckled Herbert to himself.